How Flexible Are You?

Contents

Written by Ashley Marks

Running, Jumping, Bending, Stretching

Gymnast tumbling

Did you ever watch a gymnast tumbling?
Did you ever see a jumper jumping high?

Gymnasts can tumble, and jumpers can jump
high because their joints are very flexible.

If someone is flexible, it means they can
stretch and bend their joints.

Gymnast bending

Flexible People

Some people are very flexible because they have taught their bodies to do special things. Some people do lots of exercise to make sure they stay flexible.

Some people train for years and years to be able to move their bodies in special ways. Some circus performers need to be flexible. They train for hours every day to be able to perform their acts.

Circus performers

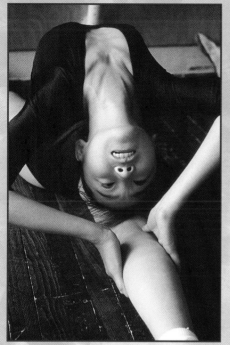

Some people are very flexible because they train hard.

How Flexible Are You?

Would you like to know how flexible you are?
Here are some tests for you and your friends to
try. You can test three different parts of your
body to see if they are flexible. Make sure you
read all the steps before you start each test.
Read the warning signs before you start.

What You Will Need

- A ruler
- A stick or a towel
- A friend

Hi!
I'm here to
remind you
to do all the
tests safely.

COACH

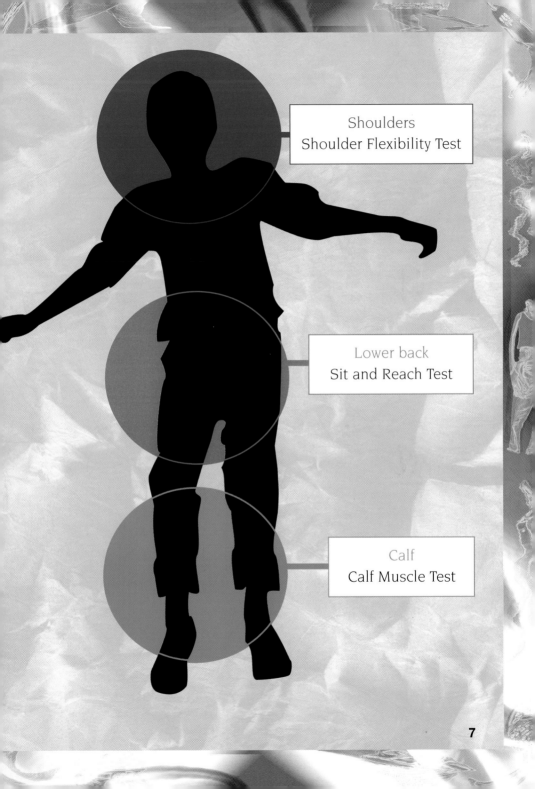

Shoulders
Shoulder Flexibility Test

Lower back
Sit and Reach Test

Calf
Calf Muscle Test

Shoulder Flexibility Test

What To Do

- Hold a towel or stick in front of you with both hands apart and facing down.

- Lift the towel or stick over your head to behind your back without letting go.

- Do the test again and again, each time moving your hands closer together. Stop when you cannot lift the towel or stick over your head without letting go.

- Ask your friend to measure how far apart your hands were when you stopped. The closer together your hands were, the more flexible you are.

Shoulder Flexibility Test

Names:	Distance Between Hands
1 Michael	
2 Amir	

COACH

Warning!

- Keep both hands on the stick or towel as you lift it over your head.
- Do the test slowly and carefully.

Sit and Reach Test

This test will tell you how flexible your lower back is.

What to Do

- Take your shoes off. Sit on the floor with your legs straight out in front. Roll up the towel and put it under your knees.

- Stretch out your arms in front. Slowly lean forward as far as you can. Have your partner check you do not bend your knees any more.

- Get your friend to measure how far from your toes your fingertips are when you have reached as far as you can. The closer your fingertips are to your toes, the more flexible you are.

Sit and Reach Test

Names:	Distance From Toes
1 Michael	
2 Amir	

Warning!

- Lean forward slowly.
- Keep your fingertips level.
- Keep your legs flat on the towel.

Calf Muscle Test

Your calf muscle is at the back
of your leg between the back
of your knee and your ankle.

What to Do

- Place one leg as far away from a wall as you
  can so that when you bend your knee it will
  touch the wall.

- Measure how far from the wall your toes are
  when you cannot move back any further, and
  still be touching the wall with your knee.

- Do the same thing with your other leg. The
  further away from the wall your toes are, the
  more flexible you are.

Calf Muscle Test

Names:	Distance Toes Are From Wall
1 Michael	
2 Amir	

COACH

Warning!
- Make sure you keep your heel flat on the floor or ground.
- Measure the distance carefully.

How Flexible Are You?

Flexibility Tests

Names:

1 Your Name

2 Your Friend

Do you think you are very flexible? Copy this chart. Rate yourself by ticking one of the boxes.

  Below average

  Average

  Above average

Distance
Between Hands

1

2

Distance
From Toes

1

2

Distance Toes
Are From Wall

1	

2	

Can you and your friend think up some more tests to measure how flexible you are?

Warning!
- Make all your tests safe tests.
- Check your tests with a grownup before you do them.

Index